TREMBLING HEARTS IN
THE BODIES OF DOGS

Also available by Selima Hill

A Little Book of Meat (Bloodaxe Books, 1993)

Trembling Hearts
in the
Bodies of Dogs

NEW & SELECTED POEMS

Selima Hill

BLOODAXE BOOKS

ISBN: 1 85224 288 4

First published 1994 by
Bloodaxe Books Ltd,
P.O. Box 1SN,
Newcastle upon Tyne NE99 1SN.

Bloodaxe Books Ltd acknowledges
the financial assistance of Northern Arts.

Cover printing by J. Thomson Colour Printers Ltd, Glasgow.

Printed in Great Britain by
Cromwell Press Ltd, Broughton Gifford, Melksham, Wiltshire.

It is with love – and the smiles
that spread across my face
when I think of her –
that I dedicate this book
to my dear friend Amelia.

Acknowledgements

This selection includes work from Selima Hill's collections *Saying Hello at the Station* (1984) and *My Darling Camel* (1988), as well as the whole of *The Accumulation of Small Acts of Kindness* (1989), all these previously published by Chatto & Windus. It includes a complete new collection, *Aeroplanes of the World* (1994), but no poems from her recent collection *A Little Book of Meat* (1993), which is available separately from Bloodaxe. A section of *The Accumulation of Small Acts of Kindness* won first prize in the Arvon/*Observer* International Poetry Competition in 1988.

Acknowledgements are due to the editors of the following publications in which some of the poems in *Aeroplanes of the World* first appeared: *Agenda, Ambit, As Girls Could Boast* (Oscars Press, 1994), *Buddhism Now, First and Always* (Faber, 1988), *The Guardian, The Honest Ulsterman, The Independent, The Independent on Sunday, London Magazine,London Review of Books The New Poetry* (Bloodaxe Books, 1993), *New Statesman & Society, New Writing* (British Council, 1993), *Poetry Book Society Anthology 1988-1989* (PBS/Hutchinson, 1988), *Poetry London Newsletter, Poetry Review, Poetry with an Edge* (Bloodaxe Books, new edition, 1993), *Proof* (Hull), *Resurgence, The Rialto, 6 Women Poets* (Oxford University Press, 1992), *Times Lit-erary Supplement, Tracks* (Dublin), *Tricycle* (USA), *What* (Canada), *The Wide Skirt* and *Writing Women*.

Some of the poems in *Aeroplanes of the World* are dedicated to friends: 'The Dog-Man' is for Janie; 'Brueghel's Helicopter' for Nicky; 'Eating Lychees in South Kensington' for Inigo; 'Carnations' for Bruce; 'Orchids' for Tom; 'Sips' for Mike Maynard; and 'Silence' is for Padraic Daly.

The title of this book refers to a drawing by Oswald Tschirtner, *Bebende Herzen In Liebe Der Hunde* (1979). This title, in turn, is a quotation from a poem, *Das Leben*, by Ernst Herbeck. Thanks are therefore due to them both. The drawing is reproduced on page 10, courtesy of Haus der Künstler Gugging. She is also grateful to the Arts Council of Great Britain for the writer's bursary awarded in 1993 to work on this book. And finally she would like to thank Sanchir, Suydun and Taivan for introducing her Mongolia where some of these poems first, in a way, began'.

The cover photograph, *Hank* by Harry Scott, was shown in the exhibition *The Animal in Photography 1843-1985* at the Photographers' Gallery in 1986. The publishers have been unable to trace Harry Scott, and want to pay him a fee for their use of his work.

Contents

Aeroplanes of the World (1994)

O. T. 1979

BEBENDE HERZEN IM LEIBE

Der Hunde

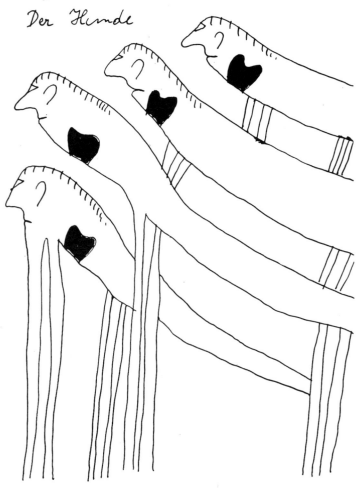

SAYING HELLO AT THE STATION
(1984)

Questioning Mr Bonnet

Mr Bonnet, the helpful Egyptologist,
explains the strange cosmology
in his *Reallexikon der ägypschen
Religionsgeschichte* that he wrote
when he was dying in Berlin:
Horus, the god of light, hid his semen
in a dish of chopped lettuce leaves,
and greedy Seth, the god of darkness,
pig-headed, metal-boned, swallowed it,
and so, by trickery, the moon was born:
Thoth, on a lotus flower, the blue baboon!

He crosses the celestial ocean
as helmsman of the world,
called Aah, the vizier of Ra, the sun.
He loads the gleaming boat
with palm leaves which record
the days and nights in notches,
for he is the measurer of time,
and he invented writing.
He carries an ivory writing palette
in his long black fingers, to instruct
the scribes who squat before him on the sand.

And he helps them on their later journey
through the Night Of A Million Years
as Thoth, the protector of the dead:
he takes them kindly by the hand
and guides them through the underworld;
his nine baboon musicians line
the long bank where the travellers
pass on their way to Osiris,
dreaming of playing draughts
with the gods and dancing with them
in the Field of Reeds.

Mr Bonnet, did you meet him, and will I,
when I step on board the silver barque?
Will he be saying *Pleased to meet you,
Mrs Hill, and how's the writing going?*
as we descend the corridors of night
into the Judgment Hall. Will he pat me
on the shoulder with his cracked
avuncular hand and, tucking my book
inside his sky-blue cape, will he wink
before he picks his tail up and climbs
onto his special perch above the scales?

Below Hekla

I appear like a bird from nowhere.
I have a new name.
I am as clean as a whistle.
I beat the buttermilk in big white bowls
until it is smooth.
I wash the pearly plates under the tap,
and fifty canvas bumpers and fifty socks.
They drip in the sun
below grey mountains like the moon's.

Each night I lift the children
in their sleep and hold out
the china pot for them:
Wilt þú pissa, elskan,
pissa, pissa I whisper
as I tiptoe from bed to bed...
Around midnight,
I go to the geyser below Hekla
and bathe in the warm water.

I am a short fat English girl.
I am twenty-five mothers.
I lead my children in a line
across the heather to the church.
The father watches me
from his dark door.
He shakes his head,
and takes me by the hand:
Blessa þú, elskan, blessa þú!

And now, September,
dust is flying: the bus is here.
I am ready.
I am on my way to Reykjavik,
Leith, Liverpool...
The children of the Barnaheimilið
are running to the gate like hens.
Goodbye, blessa þú,
give our love to the Beatles, goodbye.

14

The Fowlers of the Marshes

Three thousand years ago
they were fowling in the marshes
around Thebes – men in knotted skirts
and tiered faïence collars,
who avoided the brown crocodile,
and loved the ibis, which they stalked
with long striped cats on strings,
under the eye of Nut, the goddess of the sky.

My mother's hushed peculiar world's the same:
she haunts it like the fowlers of the marshes,
tiptoeing gaily into history, sustained by gods
as strange to me as Lady Nut, and Anubis,
the oracular, the jackal-masked.
When I meet her at the station, I say
Hello, Mum! and think *Hello, Thoth,*
This is the Weighing of the Heart.

Dewpond and Black Drain-pipes

In order to distract me, my mother
sent me on an Archaeology Week.
We lived in tents on the downs,
and walked over to the site
every morning. It was a Roman dewpond.

There was a boy there called Charlie.
He was the first boy I had really met.
I was too shy to go to the pub,
but I hung around the camp every night
waiting for him to come back.

He took no notice of me at first,
but one night the two of us
were on Washing-Up together.
I was dressed in a black jersey
and black drain-pipes, I remember.

You in mourning? he said.
He didn't know I was
one of the first beatniks.
He put a drying-up cloth
over my head and kissed me

through the linen BREEDS OF DOGS.
I love you, Charlie I said.
Later, my mother blamed herself
for what had happened. *The Romans
didn't even interest her*, she said.

Elegy for the Bee-god

Stingless bees
were bred in tree hollows
for beeswax and honey.
Every year, in the month
called Tzec, the bee-keepers
played their raspadores
and danced across the fields
with bells and ribbons
round their feet, to honour
the fat bee-god, who buzzed
in the heated air
to their music.
He lived in a gold house
in the hotlands, and drank
cocoa sweetened with honey.

All's quiet now, it's June,
and he's not here, the late,
the long-forgotten bee-god,
who sped on zigzag wings
across the sky to the faithful.
Cross-eyed, bejewelled
and tattooed, drumming
his fluffy yellow feet
on the tree hollows,
he gave the bees new hope,
and cocoa sweetened with honey.

If ever I find him – thin,
justly offended, dead
in the dry chaparral –
I will put jade beads
and honey on his tongue,
and wrap him in a shroud
of wings, and loop his neck
with pearls from Guatemala;
I will light him candles
of beeswax, bringing sleep,

and he will rest in the shade
of the First Tree,
and wait for me there –
humming a tune, and drinking
cocoa sweetened with honey.

The Ram

He jangles his keys in the rain
and I follow like a lamb.
His house is as smoky as a dive.
We go straight downstairs to his room.

I lie on his bed and watch him
undress. His orange baseball jacket,
all the way from Ontario,
drops to the floor – THE RAMS, in felt,

arched across the hunky back.
He unzips his calf-length
Star-walkers, his damp black Levi's,
and adjusts his loaded modelling-pouch:

he stands before me in his socks –
as white as bridesmaids,
little daisies, driven snow.
John Wayne watches from the wall

beside a shelf-ful of pistols.
Well, he says, *d'you like it?*
All I can think of is Granny,
how she used to shake her head,

when I stood by her bed on Sundays,
so proud in my soap-smelling
special frock, and say *Ah,*
Bless your little cotton socks!

The Flowers

After lunch my daughter picked
handfuls of the wild flowers
she knew her grandfather liked best
and piled them in the basket of her bicycle,
beside an empty jam-jar and a trowel;
then, swaying like a candle-bearer,
she rode off to the church
and, like a little dog, I followed her.

She cleared the grave of nettles
and wild parsley, and dug a shallow hole
to put the jam-jar in. She arranged
the flowers to look their best
and scraped the moss from the stone,
so you could see whose grave
she had been caring for.
It didn't take her long – no longer
than making his bed in the morning
when he had got too old to help her.

Not knowing how to leave him,
how to say goodbye, I hesitated
by the rounded grave. *Come on*,
my daughter said, *It's finished now*.
And so we got our bicycles and rode home
down the lane, moving apart
and coming together again,
in and out of the ruts.

Ty-Coch

And now the snow has fallen
over the house where we were lovers
and the weight of the snow
has made the roof cave in.

They have taken away the timbers,
and put the bed out on the terrace
where the roses used to grow.
Snow surrounds the house

in drifts, like bears;
and sheep, come down off the mountain,
shelter in the room
we used to love in.

Chicken Feathers

I

What a picture!
She has tucked her wild-looking chicken
under her arm and stares out
over what seems to be a mountain pass
on a windy day.
She is wearing a blue linen dress
the colour of summer.
She reminds me of Brunhilde – alone, bronzed, unfamiliar.
She doesn't look like anybody's mother.

II

She used to love dancing.
She went to the Chelsea Ball
dressed as a leopard;
there she met my father,
who looked so dashing
in the Harlequin suit
his tailor made for him
from raw silk.
He had tiny shoes
like Cinderella's.
I have seen them.

III

She comes to collect me from school,
on time, silent,
and I hand her my coat and satchel –
avoiding, even then, her lovely eyes,
that look down on my world
like distant stars.
I play with the girl next door,
and don't come home till bed-time.

IV

From the lighted window
I watch my mother
picking leeks in the twilight.

I will have soup
for my supper,
sprinkled with parsley.

She passes me my creamy bowl.
My hands are warm,
and smell of soap.

My mother's hands are cold as roots.
She shuts up the chickens
by moonlight.

V

How can they think I am asleep
when he bends down and kisses
the nape of her neck,
and goes away to his own room,
while she sits in front of her mirror
and brushes and brushes
her waist-long silver hair?

VI

The hens are all gone.
How happy she used to be
setting out in her long tweed coat
across the orchard
with her bucket.
Chuck, chuck, chuck, she called
and they'd all come running.

VII

She walks behind the hedges
of the large garden, stooping
from time to time
to pick narcissi
for her mother's grave,
now that it is Easter.
We don't want to go.
We're too young to remember
our grandmother –
and besides it will be cold
in the grave-yard
where the wind blows
straight in off the downs.

VIII

He went to his room with an orange
in his hand, and died there
sometime during the afternoon.
My mother spent the day in the kitchen.
When I came in from the garden
I was sent upstairs
to call him down to tea:
he was sitting by the window
with his back to me.
On the table beside him
were four boats made of orange peel,
with the pith piled neatly inside them.
My mother couldn't stand up.
She kept on saying she was sorry,
but she couldn't stand up.
It must be the shock she said.
It wasn't grief.
Come and sit down she said,
And have your tea.

IX

Tonight I kissed my mother,
for the first time that I can remember;
though I must have kissed her before,
as all daughters kiss their mothers.

She was passing in front of me
to kiss the children, and I leant down
and touched her cheek with my lips.
It was easy – like the lighting of a candle.

X

My sister always says
that on the morning our father died
he was working on a drawing of a liner
disappearing over a white horizon.
She says it is a symbol.
She's got the picture by her bed.
I would rather think of dying
as a coming into harbour,
a sort of final mooring.

XI

You put in at a little jetty.
There is someone there to welcome you –
not sinister – but rather surprising –
someone you know. In front of you rise
banks of fern and shining celandines.
You can smell the woods.
They are full of life,
but very still.

XII

My mother and I, in our way,
understand each other.
When I kneel by her grave,
in need of a little consolation,
I will picture her standing
on a hillside in bright sunlight,
lifting her hand to wave to me;
or is she brushing away the feathers
that drift like dreams into her hair
and tickle her cheek, till she smiles?

MY DARLING CAMEL

(1988)

The Holidaymakers' Daughter

It doesn't matter what she looks like.
She's in one of her moods again,
and her parents, God bless them,
have driven off in their old Ford,
leaving her alone
on a rock overlooking the sea,
with the key to the bungalow,
in case it starts to rain,
and something to eat
in the fridge.
It doesn't matter, her mother had said,
but her father was red as a beetroot.

She will uncurl in her new-found solitude
like paper flowers from Japan
that grow when you put them in water.
She will develop
a kind of passionate detachment,
like a hen. (At night she reads
The Elegant Sayings of the Lamas –
'a hen when at rest produceth
much fruit', that sort of thing.
She tries not to see the hen
too literally, but to get a feeling
of purity and earnest calm.)

Father Biddy, The Horse-Guard Priest –
who was he, she wonders,
with his shaven head and long black skirts
and his grey that he galloped at dawn?
She did know one priest, Father John.
He visited the Pet Cemetery
when she was doing the flowers,
but he was fat, and holding his hand
was like holding a helping of trifle.
He hid pennies in his habit
and asked the girls to find them.
She couldn't learn peace of mind from him...

I need a father, she concludes,
who would find it perfectly natural
to roll my body into a ball
and leave me in peace in a sandy cave
like the mummy of Uan Muhuggiag...
She's just nodding off on her warm rock,
a neat furry bundle
smelling of aniseed and myrrh –
not 'unfurling' at all,
or feeling 'nice to live with' –
when she hears the Ford
backing into the lane,

and picks up her binoculars
as if she's watching the birds.

The Significance of Significance
(i.m. Dorothy Richards)

She was worried he couldn't be happy
just loafing about by the river,
like she liked doing.
Plans, and plans about plans, and sex,
was *his* idea of happiness.
He wore a floppy hat.
She felt so lonely!

Another thing, she couldn't spell.
Laborinth. Itiniry. Elann.
She cooked him cockles
in a thick orange sauce,
and bought him a suitcase –
'for the Great Man'.

They sat on a rocky mountain
dressed in leather.
Sardines and beer.
Parois vertigineuses.

Their children were his books.
She understood that.
O Significado De Significado,
lecture notes.

'The blissfully well-run nursing-home'
is now public knowledge –
her little lump, like longing,
prized from her oesophagus;
her crawling from the hut
on her knees.

A tortoise-shell comb,
embroidery,
The Crack.
A lovely moth.
'The nurse is a crashing bore'
...poking about among her mysteries.
God bless you, Patty.

Queenio

Sand the risen peach, swollen with lust,
introduce a finger-nail tentatively
under its congested lip;
the juice will coil down her wrists
and lonely open hips, restless,
engorged with maggots. *Please come home.*

Lust has turned her hidden milk to bone.
Peach-blossoms stiffen,
goat-thick orchards sink,
eyed beetles wink and push like hounds
against her skin; *peach-girl, don't go.*
Shaky, untouchable, defiled by desire,

she casts around for somewhere soft to lie.
Come here. The knee-deep fruit play Queenie
with her loving soul, stripped clean
and tranquil by the coloured mouths
of peaches soft as eiderdowns.
They whisper *Queenio.* I said *Come here.*

Peggy

He loved the sunlight –
this was in New Mexico –
he loved the sunlight,
and he used to go for long walks
with the llama, Peggy;

and when his mother died,
one night in June,
he brought the llama with him
to the funeral:
standing like a queen in the mist,

batting her long eye-lashes
like cream.
His mother died
to get away from them!
She suffered terribly.

He used to be a tailor
like his father –
pricking his pot-belly with the pins
and sucking the redcurrants
that he made.

His mother was a gold statuette.
He wanted so much love,
that was the trouble,
yet, if you tried to smile,
he looked away.

The llama called him
Chocolate Eyes.
She said, *Don't cry.*
She was the only thing
he wanted in the end.

Natural Wonders

I

The lovely boy
washes himself all over

in a ski-hut. His mother sends
a new suit every year.

'He only cares about
his mathematics.'

II

He's tired.
He hates the snow.
He can't stop masturbating.

Each little death,
each floating point cries
Heaven, where are you now?

III

The handsome mountain-dwelling monk lies dead.
Something is wrong with the electric fan.

His secret love-affair
exceeds his wildest dreams,

while here on earth
the other monks are lapsing.

NOTE: *In the technical term 'decimal floating point', the*
sequence 2658 13, for example, would be used to represent
the number 7.658 x 1013, or 26580000000000.

Lotty

A white South African depressive
is kneeling on the veldt in Waterberg
training the beam of an electric torch
onto a little garden, where a king and queen
in white are watering their fungi-beds.
Baby soldiers wriggle on the paths,
and lift their heads from time to time
to suck the lovely globules forming
on the queen's black jaws...

He kneels by the nursery all night.
It's true he isn't well.
His wife died, and he lived alone
with Tame Toktokkie X and Tame Toktokkie Y.
His six-inch mother scorpion,
who carried sixteen babies on her back
in pairs, died recently as well.
He used to call her Lotty, or Carlotta,
his mother's and his grandmother's name.

Lucy

They lie down naked in the spider room
where legs are ears. They listen as they spin.

Then Lucy takes him for a walk. My dear,
in half an hour, she is in love with him.

Ulrike Meinhof, sing angelically;
Mongol invaders, bathe in padded light;

it is the Buddha passing on his elephant.
Lucy, take your love and follow him.

Benjamin

I am so close
I could kiss you, Benjamin.
(Our eyes never meet.)
Do you remember
slicing shins like fruit?

Do you remember
stepping through the snow
with nothing on?
(I'm pulling off your jeans.
I'm very close.)

You dance and hide
and live on peas
like necklaces.
(She wishes you would smile,
but you don't.)

You're sleeping on the floor
beside your *ra*
where crow-black songs
revolve, revolve, revolve.
(Your mummy thinks you are a sort of ghost.)

A Skiing Accident

Even the humble mole
dreams while he sleeps,
a little man as clean as a tomato.
Lives in hills, dreaming of a beetle coming in.

The presidents
dream of the presidents,
breaking their hearts on the piste.
Pineapple Lip Balm. Blood on her mitts.

The Seashore House

The sound of waves
comes creeping through the house
to stroke the sullen waters
of the garden, and my body,
like a stone, beside the garden,
begging, begging to be left untouched,
because she's bruising me:
may all her slow attempts
at getting close to me
fly off into the sound of waves
like birds with rock-grey wings!
I lie as still as someone
balancing a bowl of fruit
or rabbits on their head.

Beside the pond my dog
is gnawing bones
that crawl with ants,
and every now and then he stops
to rub his lips and nose
along the grass
that closes over him.
This afternoon aches
like a bell,
the sea is slow,
and if you come and look for me
beside the pool of melted water
you will find a stone
as cold and passionless as silk.

Silk is the liquid stone
my mother wore,
I see it slipping, slipping, like a skin;
I wear a scarf myself sometimes, I know,
to hide the scar
my mother made
I do not want to show:

my mother is afraid of love
and I, her silver-skinned
burnt only daughter –
tissue-head, peculiar, queen of pain –
I cry for kisses like she cries for shame.
The sound of waves
comes creeping through the house.

Early Nights

When people asked her
what her secret was,
she always answered
Early Nights.

She came upstairs
before I was asleep myself
sometimes, wearing a pair
of blue silk pyjamas.

I couldn't get to sleep
because the thought of silkworms
making silk in little boxes
gave me nightmares.

We had a magic word –
Przewalski
Przewalski –
to make them go away.

Przewalski was a captain
who was mad about Mongolia,
and trained wild horses
to 'die' for him.

Darling,
she used to say,
if praying doesn't work,
imagine visiting the zoo:

feel the lovely elephant,
the antelope, the gnu.
They sleep by the canal.
Recite their names.

It never works.
The captain
is a cruel man,
and I can't pronounce his name.

The Unsuccessful Wedding-Night

It's all because of Buster.
Of course, it's unreasonable,
he couldn't possibly have come –
his barking, his midnight walk,
the way he scratches at the blankets –

but as she presses her face
into the pillow of the small hotel,
she can't help missing him
terribly. She imagines the two of them
hiking in bright sunshine

over the Western Ghats; and soon
she begins to whimper to herself,
her runny nose trailing
over the foam pillows
like the Vasco da Gama of snails.

The Ptarmigan Hunter

I

I'm being kept awake
by too many kisses

and the new central-heating system
of a high-rise Carousel hotel.

The hot pipes go *tick tick*
and this man I hardly know

keeps turning me over and over
like the hunter on the radio

who came across a mummy
while on holiday in Greenland.

II

Lady of Qilakitsoq,
sleeping on ice,

your face tattooed
by the old woman

with the seal-bone needle,
your body wrapped

in cormorant ṣkins
and polar willow leaves,

sleep
while you can.

III

An off-duty ranger
drove over in his Dodge from Umanak

to shoot ptarmigan,
and found a young woman, freeze-dried,

like coffee, under a rock.
He cut off her black underclothes

and took them home to his father
who, being afraid of ghosts,

fed them into the Garbage Guzzler
he had just bought.

The Bath

He presses an oval of soap
into the palm of his hand
and twirls the bristles in the violet foam

until it quilts his fingers like the snow
where trappers crawl to pull the hairs
from little Russian weasels.

I lie under the greying water; drape
my flannel on my curls
like palls, or like the coloured coats

that poodles wear; or muslin
lain on cheese in dingy larders
to protect it from the flies.

Not that he's likely to look:
his only joy's his – twizzle twizzle twizzle –
obsessive pirouettes. Then I remember

He's been dead for weeks.
I roll over in the water thoughtfully,
feeling – not lonely exactly –

more like a floating pear-half
having warm chocolate sauce poured over me.

Mother Stone

My father was a tall man who approved of beating,
but my mother, like a mother stone,
preferred us to be sitting in a small room
lined with damson-coloured velvet
thinking quietly to ourselves, undisturbed;
everything was slow and beautiful
when we were being punished: all we had to do
was watch the dark-red petals' roses
press against each other in a slight breeze
on the window pane, and blossoms fall
in silence from the cherry tree;

and now my son is lying in a long white shirt
across our eiderdown, trying to stay awake,
and fingering my spine's shell pink as if I were a beach
and he were blades of marram grass in drifts of sand.
I dab my face with cream that smells of cucumber
and whisper in a distant milky voice
Of course I'll wake you up when he comes;
and then his eyelids close,
and in his self-created darkness he is following
a big car on a motorway at night,
it turns into the driveway to the house,
and presently the driver gets out:
it is only a bear in the moonlight,
walking on the lavender beds.

Eating Chocolates in the Dark

And after that, the diaries stop.
We think he went to his grandmother's,
whom he adored apparently.
They sat on her bed
with the lights turned off,
and ate chocolates,
and listened to the sea.
It was a kind of ritual
they both found very comforting.
Her other love was hyacinths.
He said he didn't like them,
and asked her to take them away.

And then he started telling her
about a lost eskimo
who paddled up the Don in a kayak.
He was dressed in sealskin,
and very tired. After a few days,
he caught a cold and died.

The dip dip dip of the little boat,
and his sad story-telling voice,
were like a lullaby,
and she was asleep, or nearly asleep,
when suddenly he asked her
if she believed in God.
(She told me all this quite openly –
the old Russian grandmother,
half lying back on her cushions.

Perhaps I shouldn't say this, she said,
but listen to me for a moment –
if you wake up,
and feel something fat like a puppy
wriggling between your legs,
you're not going to say it's God,
or the answer to all your questions,
or Love, are you? It's sex!
It was the same for him.)

No one

No one is to touch me
but the Lord.

His fingertips caress me
like a knife.

Everywhere I go
I am adored.

I want to be a monk
but I'm a wife.

Not All the Women of England

At the top of the bank
a blond airman
is doing sit-ups
in the tenderest
of early-morning sun.
I want to squash him flat.
He's like my Uncle Pat's
gold cigarette-case
that flies open
when you touch it.

You cruise along the fence
with your elbow
on the rolled-down window-edge.
Everything you come near
falls to bits.

The cattery sells bedding-plants
and runner-beans.
Someone has been up here
to mow a tiny lawn,
and hang a sign above it,
opposite the fence I mentioned
and the bank, before the airman came.

The passenger, the passenger,
I don't want to be the passenger.
Please can we stop at the Trout Lakes.

You came into my bedroom
carrying a duck,
and we lived together happily
for five years.

(She was so tame,
they wrote about her
in the *Whitby Gazette*.)

And now you're driving a saloon
I've come to hate
round and round the camp
like a bum.
I think I'm going to say
I want to leave you.
I want to leave you.

The hearts on the shutters
make the houses look like
cuckoo-clocks, or little chalets –
can you hear the cow-bells tinkle? –
where Mother Bear and Father Bear
eat fondue. They overlook
the fence and the bank.

The airman walks away
to living-quarters
we can't see
like a zoo animal.
He polishes his boots.
He's far from home.
Deep in trout lakes on the other side
trouts' dreams of flies
come true...

Not all the women of England
are boiling kettles
by the tall gates
but I love them all.
They shelter in the oaks
on the soft verges
where the airman lights up
his king-size cigarette.

Jacko's Girl

Send me a real dog-faced ape
that rides a dog, and plays the harp
or lute, who goes 'la la la la'
and stands up upside-down in the park.

We'll walk round flower-beds,
through rooms of light,
looking for the room I fell in love in,
singing *Stella Maris* in my bra.

That's where the velvet monkey lived.
I wanted him. I saw his dark red fingers
crush his dress.
He was my sister Mary's doll, not mine.

My present was my first geranium,
that smelled of peppermints and had no bones.
It was a post. I wanted a baboon.
They come from Abyssinia in crates.

Ouarzazate

Flies are entering
my mouth.
They drink
at my eyes.
They love them.

I've lost my hands
so how can I
brush them away?
C'est toujours midi,
Madame.

My heart goes
boom pause boom pause boom.
Don't touch me,
je vous en prie,
or I'll kill you.

Visiting the Zoo

The tall giraffes can never sit.
Their names are Valerie and Gwendoline.

I am their tall reticulated son.
This is our sand and hay.

Follow our gold strip to holy Tassili,
blonde swallow-tails, hares, a little milk.

You are a good girl. He will never know
you are in love with someone else, not him.

The Small-Mammal House

My twin sister Mary leans against a cage
where little kinkajous are watching her with interest.

Arboreal nocturnal sort of bears
with a passion for your chocolate, I see.

All I got was bits of chewing-gum –
your 'sapodilla-gum-tree-juice-gum', chickle.

Who took the photo anyway?
You shouldn't let them when you look like that.

'*Glissez, mortels, n'appuyez-pas*, GLISSEZ !'
Remember Louli, with her ear-muff hair?

'Tippy-toes, tippy-toes, tall as you can!
Reach up to those forbidden chocolates, Mary!'

You were my elective mute, becoming almost elegant
in time to Louli's elevating music...

It isn't good to watch small mammals by the hour,
all hunched-up. Also, funny men go down there, Mummy said.

Parrots

I am surrounded by parrots.
They leave their chopped tomatoes on my head.
They pile at my feet like dying socks.

Their lettuce-coloured shoulders are so heavenly
the people at the zoo go mad about them.
One of them is looking in my eyes,

and saying, *What's the matter, Billy?* (meaning me).
Catch them, someone, take them back to Paradise,
they're giving me a terrible disease.

Looking for Camels

She followed him all afternoon,
although he didn't speak to her,
or even turn to watch her
climb the dusty road.
White moths settled on her feet.
She saw a mule
with ants inside its ear.
M'sieur, m'sieur, the children cried,
running through poppies
with silver knives... Boar droppings.
Snake country... *Of course I know*
exactly where we are.

He walked into the mountains
like a man who's on his way
to kill a dog. He didn't stop.
She closed her eyes to let a drop
of calamine run down her cheek.
Somewhere sandy, somewhere soft,
that's what he had promised her...
She wrote a letter home in her head:
There's nothing here but rock,
she began,
and his HI-TEC HI-TEC HI-TEC
footsteps in the snow.

Devotion

I

My darling camel,
I want to tell you very clearly
I feel normal.
All those years of coming here
in black with P. are over.
Say you're interested.
You're so disdainful!

II

Phlegmatic, waterless, you trot,
but sometimes pace, like bears.
Deaf goats and hens
climb up and down your neck.
We ship and slaughter you.
We drink your blood.

III

I spent the days in boxes
keeping quiet.
The blue fish on the cushions
were my friends.
And during all that time
I didn't come.

IV

And then one day, my darling,
I was your *freshly-washed injected devotee.*
I stood beside your moat
with my nurse.

V

Please kiss me with your flaccid lips.
Roam free. Sweet waters of the dayas, rise.
Your feet are like an ostrich's.
You carry gold in goat-skin water-bags.
You carry brides.

VI

At sunset, I go home with the zoo-man.
His hands are like enormous teddy-bears.

PART ONE

The In-Patient

THE ACCUMULATION OF
SMALL ACTS OF KINDNESS

(1989)

The Accumulation of Small Acts of Kindness

Italics are used here for the imaginary voices the diarist hears in her head; double quotation marks for the direct speech of doctors, visitors, etc; and single quotation marks for indirect speech or words she reads or remembers reading.

CHAPTER 1 Boys

Whatever's the point of writing it all in code?
Supposing the coat is a monk,
and the sofa's a young horse;
and supposing the photos are real?
Darling, I love you.

I want to stay here in the dark for ever.
Everyone, don't talk and move around.

'A strange lamented artist who loves dancing.'
Somebody's clock. I hate her. Cold white lines.
Cut light in concave triangles, the door,
the side of the door, the panel's lonely back.
I think I am a sponge. I think I'm going.
Or shall I write in code again? Who cares.

She was descending like a boneless swan.
I wish more people would descend like that.
She knows I'm writing about her. Now she's gone.
Mr C. is calling. Here I am,
hidden in my wooden hold of doors.
Last night G. told me everything. It's true:
I will always remember you, G., I really will.
I wanted to tell you about... I nearly did.

She asked me if I masturbate. Wet grass.
Hepburn – 'fragile, feminine' – please die.
Rays of light returning on themselves.
Glossy prints of Rudolf Nureyev.

Taut purity of virgins in white landscapes,
overwhelmed by tenderness.
Don't go.
"Like drugs –" he said, "the same basic principle."
'Rebellion itself's a form of love.'

Obsession with counting birds.
My lips are aching.
They have taken away my Lord.
The Head is calling.

Marine crustaceans' seven leg-like mouths.
Goodwin's MOODS AND TENSES. Pipe tobacco.
'Little did the author know.'
Plisetskaya.
I wonder if I'm good at telling lies.
'Un homme secret, il danse dans la rue.'
I do not know the rules.
Oh yes you do!

"What's she really like?"
She is a virgin.
Yellow parrots, lettuce, nylon wool.
I went back to the study after supper.
The bluebells are in session in the woods.
Wearing dresses frightens me.
Calves.
Nipples.
The teachers smell of beans and dressing-gowns.

The dark proud gentleness of feathers
reflected in the dancer's famous face.
Her hair is gold. She hates the other partner.
Black satin, tinsel, armaments unfold.
She didn't know she made me cry. I told her.
Broad hands. Dark blood. A little rice and milk.
Down down down to the creator
of diamonds and coal and roots in silver tights.
Beaten cut tormented killed and counter-killed.
This isn't what you think. It's radioactive.
Many men and unknown things go down there.
Won't write about the walk. Past. Frozen colour.

Noises echo through the whitened squares.
'Mauriac choisit Emmanuelle.'
Hiding during meals – the seventh day.
I won't be watched so much by people later.

'Slowness Is Beauty' – always at top speed.
"I simply came to see if you're alright..."
'Suppressed depression, iron will' – that's me!
"You'll burn your journal next year – DEFINITELY."
Her fatherland. Tormented hope. Horned tree.

'Albert Schweitzer – famous bearded saint,
authority on Goethe and musician.'
'A policeman drags away a limp protester.'
'It is difficult to assess how far the jazzman
"sends" himself in the course of any session.'
The best thing they could do is to invent
a nice white dye that they could dye us with.
'Early evening in Trafalgar Square –
police begin their long removal job.'
MYSTERY MAGAZINE. I want a letter.
Writing a list of the people I have kissed – no,
writing a list of the people who've kissed me.

I have not been in Hall for eighteen days.
Chicken, peaches, cheese.
I don't know why.
'Some of the young Germans taking part
rebuild the vestries of the old cathedral.'
I want to go to B. The grass is shining.
Why do I write his name? It isn't true.
I threw the chocolate biscuits in the bushes.
Everyone is eating.
G.'s in tears.
It is not *God* who must be good and kind.
Patients eat in teams.
The rivers wind.

My socks are blood-soaked.
Gradual shapeless gloom.
I've dreamt of it three times.
White grapes for supper.
I took them all outside.

Nobody saw.
Running when exams are over.
Paris.
I'm going to eat outside again tonight.
Frosted hay. The smell of chives and boots.
I will be sixteen in the night.
My poetry.
I want to wash my hair.
I think she's looking.

H. has got a photo. I will steal.
It's all because of H. I told you so.
Everything she's got I want.
I'll scream.

Copulation in the form of memories.
Attempts in parents' bedroom.
Cockle-shells.
'Sensible comme les bouchers.'
Banded snails.
Boys in leather jackets wait for girls.
I want it. Knees like huts. *I want it I want it.*
The Bishop of Wool. His gracious reality. Nuts.

"This doubling back she mentions seems to be
the most dynamic and influential sensation":
the door is for a long moment opened –
the timeless curling motion – sand and toes...
All I can write is *Love me love me love me.*
The unforgettable dream. The golden sand.
The unforgettable dream, already forgotten.
All I can write is gathered in my hand.

He was kissing a different woman every time.
I don't know how to laugh. *Hilarious laughter.*
'Dans le petit berceau peint en blanc,
il attendra le retour de Belmondo.'
Still telling me I write too much. I know.
'Who saw in death love's dark immaculate flower.'
They don't warm slippers. Painted houses. Grass.
I don't know where I'm going. Frothy water.
The sound of pouring coal and barking spaniels.
'*Et sur vos lèvres meurent les Caratines.*'

Cows sitting down.
White sugar.
Being in love.
And when one starling leaves,
they all fall over.
The road, the frost, the pram, the spinning spokes.
Two sumptuous new creations drench my body.
Headmistresses adjust their iron gates.
Tearing out the bits about themselves.

The tired Indian waiters slip in snow.
"She calls my girlfriends 'lodgers'."
Concubines!
Words like cats.
Compulsion to repeat.
I smell delicious.
Swimming. Feel my skin.
It is confined to small remoter pools.
'Artists lie most when they tell the truth.'
'A way of life commensurate with their beauty.'
'*Sie lebten mit ihrer Mutter in einer Sandgrube.*'

She was actually giving away the man she loved.
The letter had been opened. Full of pictures.
The road was blocked. They told us to use ladders
specially painted for us by the nurses.
We had to walk through lighted farm buildings.
I don't mean any harm.
My eyes are open.

The bus-conductor says I'm looking kinky.
The poet is God's spy, his velvet cushion.
'... and if not Love, then a very strong desire
to see you RIGHT HERE NOW !'

Cake, golden syrup.
Shouting at the pool.
Don't try to come.
Music pursuing something.
Breaking glass.
Hope D. won't try to come.
It's all gone wrong.
His apartment, his trousers, his books,
his nutmeg smell.

She says why don't I ever brush my hair.

One of my most likely days. Hot weather.
DOMINI EST TERRA 24
Being pregnant makes me feel dishonest.
Now I sleep with foreign men in dreams.
My hand froze on her neck, the dancer said.
Sigmund Freud, I know you can see my knickers.

Long hot babies sleep in ticking taxis.
Compulsive rhyming.
Please don't start again.
Talking in bed. The tranquil bay. The ponies.
Her pale breasts like fish. "No, she's not here."
Pulverous or ductile; not metallic.
Totality of perfect rest.
Afraid.

Ginger ale, paddling, menstruation.
No one but my foe to be my guide.
Hampstead in the autumn, lost for ever.
Wash face, clap hands, cut paper, telephone.
Lie around, read letters, think of sex.
It's snowing and she's cut her perfect hair.
And feared his hopes and hers and all were perished.
He thought about me when I was away.
Virginity – a hive of honey bees.
Four-minute warning.
Pleats.

His sticky fingers.
The blankets are our summer. '... As ful ofté
Next the foulé netlé, rough and thikké,
The rose waxeth souté and smothé and softé...'

The little ring, the little ruthless lover
who let himself in through the rosy door.
Being good in bed.
Lost by the river.
'Attach yourself to beings, not ideas.'
Hens engender warm simple relationships.
"Your hair-style – what do you call it?"
Mystic grace.

'All your hopes are substitutes for sorrow.'
Distant mountain animals lie dead.
D. is ringing soon. What did I feel like?
He ate his soup in silence like a barge.
Sitting on the steps of the Corn Exchange,
their handbags on their knees.
I think I'm bleeding.

Both the cats are miaowing. We won't feed them.
We think it's much more fun than being kind.
A man in a suit is waving from a sports car.
If only my hair was straight.
The sun is blind.

Exaggeration of physical contact in public.
But what is the point of saving time? she said.
Training a flea. 'Nehru is dead.' Eternity.
"You know your mother thinks you're very ill."
Daddy-long-legs, alder flies, small wasps;
the undulating membrane; we inhale.
Mogadon-entranced, the loving comes.
Chi-chi adores collapsing. Shut the door.

Night positions not so bad. The field.
So this is what it's like!
Our being grounded.
I'm going to be so calm. Christ. Tell the doctor.
I'll catalogue it truly if I do.
Address is very long. What shall I wear?
The grey-green twilight infiltrates my hair.
O Mother, O Mother, provider of comfortable jerseys,
I feel the cold night air ascend the lawn.

Eight babies have been brutally attacked.
The day I saw the nurse, her cheek was bleeding.
His hair was very dark when he was born.
Orange tulips polished by the midwife.
It's silly to be frightened. Look, it's cosy.
He wore his little bonnet which I hated.
She knows when they are crying 'for attention'.
I thought I loved him more than all the rest.

She comes indoors and tidies up his toys.
She puts his cockatoo beside his chair.
She plays him music while he's in his bath.
She told me not to leave him, but I did.
I am the Mother from the Baby Ward.
He's screaming for the breast from which he's torn.

Trixie loves sweet tea.
She rides big horses.
She thinks the ballet dancer's really nice.
The circulating phosphorescent nurses,
stubbing out her endless cigarettes,
whisper things I promise not to tell her.
Trixie darling, rolled in wincyette.

When her daughter left, she kissed the window.
Mary, Mary, go to Intensive Care.
Women walk in different ways with baskets.
One of them's my mother. *Please don't laugh.*
Freshly washed, injected by the nurses,
I fold my lemon candlewick. Goodbye.
She waited for me patiently in VISITORS.
Seven years they said she waited there.

My breasts are rocks of milk.
They found the razor.
The orange flowers kicked the jug again.
Repeated fish are cruising round the curtains.
The giraffes are really nuns.
"She's so fucked-up!"

There's the rabbit, there's the coat I knitted him.
My breasts hang down and brush his lips like pears.
The Sister says I don't look like a mother.
Every day I hear his little prayers.

Little cubes of bread and peanut-butter.
He keeps on falling off the bed.
Don't cry.
The tiny boy the nurse is wheeling in
was seven inches long when he was born.
He's lying underneath his yellow teddy;
he never lets it go; he never smiles.

We like it here. It's cool. I stroke my nightie.
We're going to eat our ices at the zoo.
My socks are blood-soaked but it doesn't matter.
The night nurse is a little baby too.

The babies smell of custard tarts.
Deep breathing.
The after-coming head.
Collapsing wives.
The nurse came in to make my bed. She's knackered!
Milk and blood will cloud the tepid bath.
Fluffy babies make their mothers love them,
fast asleep with prune-juice in their hair.

The gorilla's house is dark.
He wants his biscuits.
He seems to hover on the verge of tears.
We never feel cold.
We are The Mothers.
Found at last, our babies on her knee.

I told him not to hit her but he did.
Who is that little boat for?
Not for me.
Beetroot. Boiled egg. A bowl of custard.
Elephants.
THE SEA OF GALILEE.

I stopped the car, and saw it was a baby.
At first I thought it was a little dog.
I wrapped it in a coat and brought it over.
"He ought to be much quieter, oughtn't he?"

The children are asleep like little bags,
the tulips are as sweet as marzipan,
the cabbages are blue,
the house-boat's red.
The shaggy dog, once so devoted, 's dead.

The sound of heavy boots on the gravel.
It would have been unbearable, I know.
Smoking rollies on the day-room roof-top.
"The first thing that she did was bite the nurse."
I must assume a normal public face.
"She's been here since July."
My eyelids close.
Once D. came in and saw the new day breaking.

My uterus is like a sunlit knife.
He's got a nice big face, I don't know why.
He doesn't smell like us, but of potatoes.

He's like a plum fished out of milky custard.
Endless cries of birds.
The sound of hoeing.

Whenever a child is born, a woman is wasted.
We do not quite belong to ourselves.
Crushing all the hollyhocks with teddies,
the wa-wa babies stumble: "Lift me up!"

You see, it is so lonely I get serious.
Dream of a dream and shadow of a shade.
'The writer's instinct is essentially heartless.'
The wa-wa babies burst into floods of tears.

Cherry nougat for the *quiet* children.
Fond memories –
milk jelly,
sunny weather.
It's far away, and we don't notice it,
or if we do, we don't tell anyone.

We run away and live on bread and chocolate
hidden in the bottom of our prams.

CHAPTER 3 Doctors

Miles away from anywhere,
like fish.
I want to see a doctor.
I'm in bed.
The boy is tired but happy in the moonlight.
I saw some, falling faster, stuck with blood.
I sleep curled up like shrimps in the darkness.
I long for scenes where man has never trod.
A less soft but a straighter whiteness rises.
Mother Water, I'm your baby now.
A bedside light emits a stream of questions.
Do not console me. I am not your friend.
The yellow flip-flap of the alhatross.
Now snow is filling up my little head.

Like a butcher, deep in rubber buckets,
tearing the hearts from cows' defrosting blood.
Stuck in one position like a statue.
You never lift a finger.
Sunlit bone.
Illuminated gloves. They killed my kitten.
He was the shyest man I ever met.
I wish I was a nice friendly person.
I wonder why he's dirty.
Let's go home.

My father used to sleep in the stables.
My mother knew at once when I made love.
The man who is a bird smokes No. 6's.
"Put your empty packet in the bin."
The nipples floating in the soup are carrots.
My father's got a hornet on his chin.

Far out, the lonely golfers start to cry.

The anorexic suffocates in chocolate.
My father wears a woolly cardigan
with lozenges of fear inside the pocket.

Seafarers gently drift across the ocean
with dogs and chickens in their long canoes
and colonise the islands east of China.

He said it was his wedding. It's not true.

I thought you'd be so pleased –
I shot the rabbits!
Strips of striped pyjamas soaked in tea.
The bulldog's blood drips on the red linoleum.
Her fingernails jump about like fleas.
I think they are thinking of Anna,
washing cherries.
He thought he was a goose.
I'm not surprised!
The driver's going so fast they'll all get flattened.
Beaded whisks of tails to swat fat flies.

Lying on the kitchen floor to hug him.
The doctor should be here any minute.
The yellow parrot saying *What a pity*.
Now his watch is ticking in my ear.
It's true he was my lover. *What a pity*.
The sun needs hearts of warm blood every day.
We're old enough to sleep here in fine weather.
Gertrude Bell has linen-covered thighs.
Jealous of the hands that touched the breasts
he was the first to marvel at. *Don't worry*.
So easily you'd think he's used to it.
The light that fills the world sleeps in my bed.
Waking up from dreams of frozen valleys
and violet bluebells nodding by the pools.
The face of God the doctor said I touched.
And loneliness in pink kneels down to pray.
The bedrooms house a family of camels.
"I hate to see a coffee getting cold."

The doctors say I read too much.
They're staring.
Her mouth is stuffed with custard-yellow wool.

He always hates the girls that he has slept with.
The Psychiatric Unit white with snow.
The red-haired nurse spent all day in the day-room
although she was off-duty.
How do you know?
Enormous jerseys and no knickers. Sand.
Crystallised rose-petals. Ashes. Sheep.
We watched the moorhens treading through the tree-tops,
their big green feet like camels'.
Itchy skin.

Is she quiet and listless all the time,
or is there something I should do, she wondered.
Sitting looking utterly defeated,
fingering the books she's not allowed.
The bullfinches, the bats, the precious letters
gobbled up for nothing.
Go away.

The same good-looking man who liked my cardigan.
Or is that just my illness?
Fairy cakes.
The shaggy remains of a star give sweet instruction
to sleepless lovers.
"What does he mean – he's '*going*'?"
I want to scream and scream and all I do
is write *I want to scream* down in my book.
Fathers coming closer like the tide.
One word.
Enclosed by hate.
I feel like string.
Apricots. Gold. Massed ascensions. Jam.
They're coming now. They're going to flood my veins.

The patients rise like early morning milk.
The planets' movements alternate the tides.
The waiting-room. It frightens me. The hole.
DISEASES OF THE MIND. Pet monkeys. Silk.

Wild bees know little joy.
No visitors.
I've wanted to go home all my life.
Moving deeper into purple woodland.
Lop-eared rabbits, walnuts. Wearing boots.
Ginger weasels cross the gated road.
The little dog is limping.
So am I.
My mother says I'm hopeless.
Bits of lettuce.
The doctor wrote it down:
'Her haunted mind.'

He buttoned up the collar of my jacket
and whispered in my ear 'She's dying now.'
Boiled ham and tulips.
It was evening.
I never want to help you.
"Say Goodbye."

"I like the way you're breathless – it's erotic."
PEOPLE WHO LEAVE LONDON WILL BE SHOT.
Antibiotics. Sleet. My 'fortitude'.
That blissful state in which you feel forgotten.
To get a little carpet in our bedroom,
to go under the door, a little planed.
Afternoons of fruit and acts of kindness.
"Is it true you're not allowed a mirror?"
Your mother called and said she left your washing
crying on the disinfected floor.
A lovely lady's holding out a rabbit.
The lady smiles. The rabbit's name is Pam.
My skirt is like a lorry full of whiskers.
It makes me feel sick to think of him.
The nurse has got a rabbit. Yes, it's mine!
I love its gleaming harmony!
Apologies,
I *used* to have a rabbit I called Pam.

Voices I keep catching all the time.
A mohair cardigan. A bowl of pears.
I know she said don't listen to the voices.
I've been depressed for over twenty years.

All the baby's family are missing.
Espadrilles. Potatoes. Women saints.
Her carrycot is floating in the sea.
It's 4 o'clock. The rabbit's wide awake.
"People say it's all so free and honest."
The walls are green. "He said, 'You're schizophrenic!' "
The feeling of the nurses' hands. I'm blind.
No time for sorrow's rippling fish. I'm blood-soaked.
The corner of the day-room shines like coal.
Soon I will be better. At the moment
I live in humble darkness like the mole.

The gravel drive makes everybody stumble.
The Virgin in her wooden dress is kind.
Red roses tumble softly onto water.
The day-room smells of toffee. I don't mind.

"Loving me is not enough." He laughed,
feeling with his fingers up my skirt.
He looked into my frightened, rubber eye-balls.
He smelt of fennel, weasels, sandy dirt.

Inmates waltz at dusk at party-time.
Sitting by herself in fairyland.
"It's far too late to start remembering now!"
The smell of fennel when they move. Thick tea.
The sun is setting. It is time to start.
"Everyone admires our Christmas Tree!"

Sausages and chips and apple crumble.
Everything she does is always wrong.
The vicar gave us lovely cards and honey.
The rich girl says her father won't be long.

Fluffy hands and horses fill the sky.
I do not need a coat. *Leave me alone.*
The red-eyed doctors block the corridors
with turquoise needles tipped with Methadone.

The rocks like leopards soften in the rain.
I see myself as Jesus' private nun,
lost in the mists of time, when we were little –
mushrooms; herons; woolly bears; my mum.

I had to cross the day-room on my hands,
a silent rabbit foraging for fruit.
I dread the human voice. The doctor said
"There's nothing we can do. We need your bed."

The daily wards of underwater fame.
Swimming to the pills.
Don't say my name.

The hospital is underwater, Trixie.
To widen brains, please nail all joints loosely.

This little thing's been homeless for so long
Now say goodbye.
She won't be very long.

PART TWO
The Out-Patient

CHAPTER 1 **Masters**

I step across the white dust of the runway
towards a man with pistols for a face.
He's tall and thin with one hand in a bandage.
I hear a faint *pow-pow* of disgrace.

'Departing for womanhood.' Crap. Green velvet cushions.
The baker's sons are being introduced.
The canteen of the airport smells of pepper.
I follow him towards the setting sun.
The avenue of cacti like an elephant
shelter silent groups of staring men.
We go upstairs. His buckle scrapes the brick-work.
Lust and grief. Unusual cakes. He's kind.
I'm menstruating on a stranger's blankets.
Sorrow like a silver spool unwinds.

The sun is hot. My head is full of silence
attracting hordes of angry bees like bells.
A swallow-tail, an amber necklace, henna.
I want to be so calm. 'Devotion frees.'

People, horizontal, lit, ascending,
now declare their everlasting love
by open windows, where the tepid evening
is tempting them to cast aside their clothes.

See me see me see me in the garden.
I'm made of ants.
Whose voice is that?
It's hers.
Feel between my legs two lips like lollies,
or like a blood-hound on the verge of tears.

Talking to him in a voice as distant
as unborn daughters kneeling by my bed.

Turkish delight, brazil nuts, sweetened yoghourt.
I treasure every word I think he said.

The only men were doctors. We were dollies
put to sleep in resonating halls.

The bell is ringing like an English cherry.
Picasso in his villa touches girls.

The boots that crush the roses hear me whisper
You mustn't kiss me now. He takes my hand.
Ecstasy, which makes him feel nearer,
has made me ill. I never talk. I'm banned.

The offices are empty, only you:
a violet light, a pleated skirt, a prayer
rising in the dark then drifting downward
to join the other voices of the air;
while in the muted villa, calmed by sorrow,
someone feels a lightening of snow.
We'll move you to another bed tomorrow,
we'll move you to a place where good girls go.

Bluebells, Bovril, somebody's blind spaniel.
The bluebells shine with Daddy's violet light.

She even brought her mole with her. *Don't cry*.
She ran about the rocks till it was night.

Toast and cream. Her deep-blue velvet dresses.
I haven't told the others where I've been.

Dragonflies fly round her head in traces.
There may be someone there – we'll have to see.

Someone to talk to, cold as charity.
An analgesic and a febrifuge.

Lop-eared sheep in echoing ravines.
The tiny nun is venturing to intrude.

Lamented daughters slip away like cats;
running water; seals; grace abounding:

a crippled Coptic mother's early sorrows,
through centuries of beaten earth resounding.

The doctors say my shyness is repellent.
The shyness of the bittern. I'm alone,

living in a world where pinks and pumas
drink cherry-flavoured drops of Methadone.

The other people cut down all the trees
and vivisect the cats and toads. *Roulette*.

Making honey sandwiches. Misgivings.
The way my mother handles ducks. *Nanette*.

Even the Central Predigstuhl's West Gully
denied us shelter in its icy palace.

Irish monks in frail craft made of leather
discovered Iceland, glaciers and solace.

The golden dribbles of the butterscotch
tremble on the rubber. She can't swim.

She's singing like a lover through the water,
singing through the glass her blue-green hymn.

Crystal quartz like love from Colorado.
Sealed with rheum. The chickens' sunlit meal

scattered on the lily-pond. '*Raw, tender,
hostile, hot or bored – how do you feel?*'

I feel like a table-cloth with grazing rights;
a newt; a guinea-fowl; a tulip-head;

the listlessness of rivers' eels; bandages.
Don't tell me what you think I should have said!

My body's like a zebra's; rock-hard plums;
the glittering of quartz washed by the sea;

Dorothy Wordsworth's toothache, like a crystal;
TEACH YOURSELF KARATE; amber tea.

Measuring my sleeping lover's neck.
Chicken thighs. A greeting. *Take your time.*

Running water soothes; a little music.
I can't imagine what it's like. *Like mine.*

His hand is lying on my lap like liver.
Wiping up the blood. He's very kind.

Every little star must twinkle brighter.
The poor thing's got no breasts. *O never mind.*

Bunches of butchered seagulls. Dusky archers.
You must be someone special. *Hold my hand.*

Bit by bit, not suddenly. Peach. Barley.
I thought you were never coming. *Hold my hand.*

The handsome sleeping generals lie massacred
like beautiful white flour from Singapore.

Who but a beaten specialist would offer
to map the changes of the ocean floor?

I didn't say a word about the therapy.
The doctors deal in glitter-coated worms.

A schizophrenic dressed in silk to please him,
I part my lips like lilac, brush his sperm.

I think the nurse said she was going to shoot me.
I can't sit up. I don't know what to say.

The bead-like packing may be tiny pearls. *Hush*,
everyone loves fear. Don't go away.

The shaved and beaded Maasai mothers calmly
wash their sons in milk from special cows.

He said that if I walk along serenely,
I'm worthy of their gold and violet flowers.

They broke into my room, and I was murdered –
innocent, illuminated, rose.

I cannot touch my cup in case they see me.
My mother leaves my laundry with the nurse.

She turns the light out, leaving me in darkness,
a dumb, adored, impassive amulet:

ah, I will be so lovely in the summertime,
when Doctor parts my sleepy body's net.

The central point round which the volumes settle,
his doll is staring like the smell of gas.

He wants to be alone with me. I'm sweating.
My body will dissolve. "Can't you relax?"

Sunny days of quiet desperation.
"She misses her poor daughter still, you know!"

Sunlight. Netball. Ankle-socks. White rabbits.
Ceaseless prayer like purity of snow.

Rescued from her introverted nightmare
by seeing washing billowing on the line.

Doing certain things. "Yes, please sit anywhere!"
We sit on any surface we can find.

'Write a list of gratifying activities.'
Tomato juice makes glasses hard to clean.

Suddenly the man leans down and bites me.
The lily-pond – the carp – the bluebells' gleam.

The gods of Europe shower me with smiles,
unnerving all the men that come and stare;

I dance until my heart begins to break –
then Sister comes and makes me brush my hair.

The dog has got a little curly tail
the size and texture of a tangerine.

The bluebells are as glossy as the horses,
galloping like lust into the sea.

The penned imported camels by the villa,
like ghostly castles made of sand and bone,

lean their narrow hips against the darkness,
waiting for a love they've never known.

I am alone. Where are they? Snowy weather.
Am I allowed to write like this or not?
She said that I could go to the meeting,
and then she said that I had better not.

The girl in my room is reading ALONE WITH OTHERS.
I really feel I can't go through with this.
'Walking through a forest with a parcel.'
And all she wants is my companionship.

Chicory, cashew nuts, paper zebras.
"Why do you look so worried?" I don't know.
The voices fade. The floor is piled with cushions.
I wonder, will she speak when we're alone?

We are the children of This. This is the silence.
I haven't talked to anyone for years.
I can hear a pony's rhythmic cropping.
I can feel the wind against my ears.

"It's been a lovely friendly convalescence,
and I shall go home feeling much much better..."
It's miles getting back...but we don't care...
miles and miles... it really doesn't matter.

Larches in the forest bring the evening.
Disabled men drink milk among fat hens.
A sense of loss like violins pursues me
and will not let me sleep, the young man says.

Piano Pieces, fruit, embroidered slippers.
Struggle for what? Eurhythmy. Green and neat,
scentless mayweed, dragonflies, tall grasses
ripple in the grounds like greyhounds' feet.

The man who dances like the sea surrounds me.
I'm shivering. I'm sorry. It's so new.
The Spiritual Head of the Order's started laughing.
Piles of strawberry jam. "May I laugh too?"

As blossom fills the lawns of scented gardens,
fluttering whispers fill the patient's throat.
Love is more than simple acts of kindness:
it comes from deep within us like a note.

They play the flute until it's nearly morning.
The man who heals with sound is by my side.
My meditation's swilled with icy water
for Ahto and Vellamo, Ahto's bride.

Horses pass unseen in the forest,
a speckled bantam suddenly takes flight;
Molly, who is over eighty, 's mending
the wooden boat she painted gold last night.

"What does he mean by meditation anyway?"
She looks so lonely with her little plaits.
Secret letters. Failing to adore him.
Invisible vanilla. Roses. Cats.

The dogs are neither elegant nor handsome,
but make us feel warm when we are cold.
The sleeping monks are sailing into morning;
soya milk like cowries; silence; gold.

Tinned faces. Yellow cushions. *Love him more.*
And let your body say what you can't say.
It's just a little shower, she said, her suffering.
It's nice to know you like me. "It's OK"

She said that I could join the group tomorrow –
her tilted pools of everlasting wealth!
Someone in my dream is always smiling.
'You think it must be God but it's yourself.'

Community of nuns in Andalusia.
Colossal love like thunder. Bowls of shells.
The dancer had a giant dog called Hilda
who used to like to eat the daffodils.

The patient from the villa came to visit.
Rabbit fur, damp leaves. She didn't stay.
The Sister has retired to the country –
irises and blackbirds, flowering may.

Like mottled soap of olive-oil and soda;
Nivea; flat stones, their edges gone;
the soles of people paddling in the tide-line,
I feel I am being acted on.

Gardening gloves touch pale blue hydrangeas;
'becoming aware of myself as something known';
my dog has gone to sleep across my pillow;
'keep the mind in the middle of the tongue.'

The hooded men who follow me and whisper
have slipped away like weasels in the snow.
I too must say good-bye to the monastery.
The train is waiting. "Really, I must go!"

PART THREE

The Last Week

Friday

And all the time,
the heifers' solemn faces
are breathing by my side,
as soft as ash;
my little fire
is burning in the moonlight
that slips between the grasses
like a cat.

Saturday

The painted bows.
The silver nail-scissors.
Strips of paper in a stencilled tin.
A flannel in a bowl.
Hush. What's the matter?
Early morning sunlight, paper-thin.

My breath is like the long electric hair
of someone swinging on a high trapeze:
it sweeps the air and all the faces cry
ha; and again *ha!*
WHAT TURNS YOU ON?

Sunday

The river-bank is thick with summer flowers,
as stiff as pigs, as pink as fruit; massed flies
stroke their wings against the fluted sky
whose height, as sweet as hay, rings like an axe
and dyes the spotted cows a million blues.

Monday

At midnight we have rolls and oranges.
My hands are cold.
They make me cups of tea.
Sons and daughters, singing in the moonlight,
are drifting on their tin beds out to sea.

Ankle-bones,
peach-slices,
mignonette;
bars of chocolate,
fur:
I won't forget.

Tuesday

I'm sitting on my blanket
eating toast.
In India I starved.
I'm very fat.
Mother Teresa, Mother Teresa calling.
She wants me now.
She wants me in her flat.

Wednesday

A lame man walks for miles along a beach;
the dazzling sunlight magnifies his dreams:
a pool of blood that soaks into the pine-woods,
a bungalow, dead rabbits, skin-tight jeans.

Thursday

The afternoon
is giving way
to evening,
I help my tearful daughter
rinse her hair;
a bullfinch
in the holm oak
calmly singing;
my holiday;
Nijinsky;
ginger air.

My sleeping-bag smells sweetly
of the pine-wood,
my smoky hair and pillows
of warm stones.
The terns fly off like splinters of the evening.
I'm glad there's no one here.
Peach-slices.
Bones.

Friday

My sister has been racing someone's race-horse
across a valley in the pouring rain,
trying to forgive
our blood-stained mother
who killed her German Shepherd,
Violet.

The Minuet for Berenice is playing;
everything seems normal, but it's not:
we look as if we're drawing, but we're praying;
our studio of birds, our brotherhood.

Instant mashed potato, lettuce, Spam.
The rabbit on the plate is going shopping.
The islands of potato warm the lettuce
and stir the little virgin jockey's heart.

The Boyle Family. Walsingham. Hot water.
"She hasn't left her drawing-board all day."
The warm dog and the Little Tern run quietly
to Everlasting Light on pointed toes.

Saturday

Your voice is clear as crystal,
so is mine;
as turquoise,
divers,
steel,
turpentine.
Your fingers smell of Nivea,
it's cold,
your fingers smell of pine-woods and the sky;
you touch my hands,
you wash my eyes in water
enclosed in heated towels. *Say goodbye.*

'Every sort of pine will yield resin
for incense, violins and ballet-shoes.
The creamy tears are found in natural fissures,
or trickling from the wounds of broken boughs.'

The boats are on the grass,
the sun is shining,
the station-master tends his flower-bed.
I feel I am dancing underwater
and Christ is by my side, the dancer said.

AEROPLANES OF THE WORLD

(1994)

For Christy Moore,
from a humble but devoted fan

Being a Wife

So this is what it's like being a wife.
The body I remember feeling as big as America in,
the thighs so far away
his hand had to ride in an aeroplane to get there;
the giggles I heard adults giggling with
I was puzzled about,
and felt much too solemn to try;
buttons unbuttoned by somebody else, not me;
the record-player
neither of us were able to stop what we were doing
to turn off;
the smell of fish
I dreaded I'd never get used to,
the peculiar, leering, antediluvian taste
I preferred not to taste;
the feeling of being on the edge of something
everyone older than us,
had wasted,
and not understood,
as we were about to do;
his pink hand gripping my breast
as if his life depended on it;
the shame of the thought of the mirror
reflecting all this,
seem long ago,
yet somehow authentic and right.
Being a wife is like acting being a wife,
and the me that was her with him in the past is still me.

The Wasps

Our mother liked to feed me perfect veal;
and two invisible drops of Radiostol
were wobbled on my morning toast by Nurse –
a special little wafer, like a host.
She fed my upstairs sister next to nothing.
At least, that's what my upstairs sister thought.
And when I tried to move her head I couldn't.
And when her kitten started licking her,
bit by bit, as if she were a skyscraper
a tiny Tippex brush was painting white,
I ran into the yard to greet the wasps,
and let the licking carry on all night –
my sister on her bed, and me outside,
my naked body smeared with marmalade.

The Climbing Accident

Even in this terrible cold,
I can remember everything:

THE WONDERFUL WORLD OF HORSES,
my sister's hesitant bush.

Christ's blood was shed for us.
I've never been so happy!

The Man Man

Who is this man?
And why is time different here?

And what does he say,
with his mouth full of *r*s like blood?

He plunges his arms into rocks
and pulls out lizards.

Skinner of swifts,
sucker of brittle eggs,

easer of scented pianos
down warmed ramps,

who is this man,
and what does he promise me?

My mother stops my mouth. She says I must
never never tell him where I am.

My First Bra

A big brown bear
is knocking at the door:

he wants to borrow a dress
and matching knickers.

The smell of lilac
smothers me like wool;

beyond the lawns,
I hear my naked sister

crying in the nettles
where I threw her:

nobody else is having
my first bra.

The Dog-Man

The dog-man from next door has come to play the piano –
to pour out his syrupy notes
like a deluge of ripe, exhausted plums:
they stick in her hair
and mess up her ironed, imported, daisy-spangled cotton dress
that glares out sententiously
like one of those little flower-gardens
harbour-masters and sandwich-bar-owners
dedicate their lives to
with the kind of murderous possessiveness
small seaside towns
obssessed by being the nicest
go over the top with;
she's pressed against by plums as big as radiators,
emperors,
sweating Clydesdales,
suicide,
over-heated Japanese 'bath-houses for sexual relief'
she's read about, and puzzled over and tried not to see herself in –
plums buzzing with bright wasps
that cross and recross the precinct of her chair
like a switched-on electric fence
she can't move through.
Her eyes are glazed,
and her face could be basked on by lizards it's so still.
She's mistress of the art of frozenness,
hiding at the side of herself
like a pilgrim bathing in the Ganges
being cruised past by loudspeaker-toting boats;
like a diseased tomato;
like a brain-damaged child strapped in a van
who's watching, or anyway parked in front of,
an open-air, wrap-around, drive-in,
completely incomprehensible picture-show,
and the van has a sliding door
that might accidentally slither open any minute
and send a whole avalanche of untouchable things
that have no business to be there,
and should never be seen,

tumbling out into the open
like mutes or brains;
and at night,
when I'm nearly asleep,
I sometimes come across her –
vicious, hunched-up and incapacitated
still hugging her hairless awkward little thighs.

Selima Selima

Where does shame come from?
It comes from my hands.
Where does shame come from?

It comes from my name:
Selima, Selima.
My father gave it me.

Where does shame come from?
It comes from a waterfall
somebody's kept for years in a woollen purse.

My Life With Men

The first man I attracted
was my father,
who people said was young:
how young he is!
But actually he wasn't. He was old.
I told my little friends he was the lodger.
Next, the man who called me
Schlobovitz
and worshipped me unstintingly.
They all did.
And then the man I found upstairs in bed,
who said he was my
Unexpected Brother.
Why do people have to lie like that?

And later on I met his friend The Man.
And then another.
I was off my head.
I never loved them but I wanted to.
I wanted to so much I thought I did.
So much, in fact, I even married one,
and went to live in Manland, among Men;
where other women,
wrapped and stunned
like meat,
introduced me to the long machines
we mustn't leave
on pain of death
all day.

We mustn't walk,
or even go outside.
(If anyone's seen 'loose' –
without a car –
they're rounded up
and given clocks and pills.)
We mustn't talk –
except of course, effusively,
every time the phone rings.

Then we must.
(As long as what we say
is not the truth;
as long as who we're talking to's
a stranger.)

Our flowers
are dead.
Our animals
are headless.
Our children
are for smashing against walls.
And when the day
has done the best it can,
with well-scrubbed hands
we set our plastic clocks
and slip
like liners
into dreamless sleep,
remaining almost motionless till morning.

Crocuses

And is her father with her on the lawn?
Absolutely not.
She needs to be quite alone.
And what is she drinking, on the lawn?
Hot tea.
And what is she writing?
Things that have made her angry.
And has a certain bunch of flowers
made her angry?
Yes.

He stepped out
into the sunlight,
still in his nightclothes,
and made his way
down the hill
to the orchard.
Her first gold crocuses
were pushing up like fish
(she wanted *no one* to see them)
between striped wasps on plums.

And what sharp implement
was he carrying down with him?
Scissors.
And if he were to cut himself –
remember he's an old man now –
would she come running down the bank with sheets
to stanch the bleeding?
No, she would not.
And will she forgive him?
Never.

Three Sisters

Three sisters, like three hens, eye one another;
six hands, like sparrows, flutter up and down
making wreaths for you, the sisters' brother,
from winter flowers whose petals have turned brown,
from rosemary and basil's grey and blue,
from lavender, and ivy from the apple;
from snowdrops tied in ribbon, berried yew –
six hands like hymns; the kitchen like a chapel
where hens and rabbits wander in and out,
and flowers and fruit trees grow between the stones:
three lemons for the mousse; a lily; trout,
ten tickling fingers checking it for bones.
Chop, chop. That's it. There's nothing we can do.
A fly. A knife. The sickly smell of rue.

Joseph Beuys, Yul Brynner, Sigmund Freud, Gorbachev, Freya Stark and Me

We never mention it,
this secret scar
I was carried in the arms of the farmer
through the roar of burning wheat-fields to prevent;
that smelt like the piglets
left singeing in the hay-barn, screaming like hares;
that drove my mother to carry
painfully expressed breast-milk and sieved carrots
through the streets of the deserted city
at night in little jars, to soothe me with;
that banished me to a childhood
behind muslin;

papery, polished and thin,
like a dried flower,
or the ghostly imprint
of my mother's love,
or lack of love,
or whatever it was
that caused the accident –
so can you pretend, for all our sakes, if you can,
I've got nothing in common
with people disfigured by scars,
especially scars on the head, especially the face,
OK?

Standing Here Beside You

Standing here beside you makes me sad.
You're like a house I watch the windows of

knowing I can never go inside.
I see a woman passing to and fro

and envy her the freedom I can't have.
I only watch. And you?

You're watching too, frozen
in your prison of white flowers.

Milky

We peeled our sunburnt babies
like garlic cloves,

and the slivers of skin stayed where they fell
in air as stubbornly still as vastness and joy

locked in an oven would be;
where only the drip of the milk from your longed-for breasts,

as they pressed against the glass-stiff stiffening
of your Lycra swimsuit cups

like patiently caught fish contained in jars,
moved,

if you call it moving –
seeping, leaking,

giving the room the faint white smell of a dairy
falling asleep like a pear behind closed doors.

Maisie

She always reminds me of a heifer –
the way they bounce across the fields
on stiff gold legs, so clumsy and joyous,
as though they don't really realise
such stiff legs can't be bouncy;
with eyes that look as if they would flop out
in a thick warm chocolatey tide
if you turned them upside down –
which of course you wouldn't,
because they have their dignity,
even though they are heifers,
big virgin cow girls,
bovine shoats,
eyeing you up as if they are trying to decide
if you are, of if you aren't, a Messiah
coming to earth with a message for the world;
but then again,
they wouldn't care if you were,
and the message you neatly agree to agree to is this –
just scratching the sweetest patch of cow-coloured hair
it's ever been your pleasure
to quietly scratch.
Never before have they been in so much heaven.
Never before has everything human made sense.
But then they turn away
as if nothing had happened,
with the slow almost stepless step
of someone moving a souffle,
or balancing an altar on their head –
watch them as they wander off among the flowers,
with blankets and zafus, apricots and barley,
all stowed away between their stumps of horns.
I can even imagine Aufschnaiter's Rolex there,
that he sold to buy something to eat
one night in Tibet.
I've forgotten to mention the ringlet,
single and white,
that hangs from each tail
like a tendril
or Viennese whorl.

Potato City

Her name was Beryl.
Like the precious stone.
Bald and louche,
her job was beating children
and stuffing them in cots
that didn't fit
or stuffing chickens
down their hopeless throats.
Some of them were more than twice her size
so discipline was obviously
essential.
And discipline in fact
was her strong point.
Her pigeon-chested chest
was rigid with it.

Her colleague was a Miss
Kartoffel-Salat –
a sullen creature
Uncle P. produced
(judging by the idiotic name).
Bored? Was that it?
Bored to tears like me?
We should have gone to that
Potato City, alluded to
in your more garrulous moments,
where people with big heads
wear hats on spikes
they sink into their skulls
in special rituals
involving brewing the resulting discharge.

The atmosphere
begins to get oppressive,
and non-potatoes feel like creeping out.
In or out or up or down – who cares?
In the thumping subterranean darkness,
hot potato breasts,
potato knees,

potato knuckles
and potato cheeks
focus single-mindedly
on merry-making.
Even in the nurseries
lunar babies
butt each other with their heads
and laugh.

Beethoven's Mother

When the glazier
manoeuvres his rectangle of glass
across the street
like a slice of frozen lake,
I think of you;

when small flocks, roaming open fields
in autumn
like freed cyclamen,
on wings as thin as nasal blood-vessels,
sing as they fly,
I think of you;

and when I read that Beethoven's mother,
cooking pastries
in the back streets of Cologne,
'lulls his overwrought feelings
into tranquillity',
of course I think I'm Beethoven, with you.

The Toe

Not long after our late mother's death,
my sisters and myself, weak as we were,

decided to come down off the mountain
and settle ourselves here in the woods.

And if they come, they come. We have no fear.
Something, we're convinced, is watching over us,

something we're too small to comprehend.
All we see's, at dawn, a giant toe

we offer roses to we drag by night
across the heath among the wounded larks.

The Birds

They've closed it down, but someone is alive.
His eyes are watching for a door to move.
Once he saw, or thought he saw, tall women
running down the mountainside with oranges;
once he saw a soldier on a horse
looking up at him in disbelief;
but all he sees today is the road,
glittering and white, between the trees;
and, moving imperceptibly, like clocks,
the giant eyeless birds, unknown to science,
who come to fish on fine days in the lake.

Brides with Songbirds Tangled in Their Veils

As soon as people realised what was happening,
they opened up the mine in the mountains
and turned it into what they called a nightclub,
complete with 'rest-rooms', known as *Darkest Night*.
Not the most inspiring name, admittedly,
but then these people never claim to be.
In fact they're proud of being uninspiring.
The less I have to do with them the better.

I much prefer to go in search of nets –
creeping down the bank beyond the woods
late at night or early in the morning
and pocketing as many as I can
before the sentries wonder what I'm up to,
or, even worse, before the man appears
whose nets, like brides with songbirds in their veils,
I like so much on starry nights to plunder.

Silence

Her path, if you can call it one, is silence,
obviously quite different from our own,
and one, as I have said, that we will monitor.
It's true she makes my people here uneasy –
she makes it hard to go on acting normally,
and not to call in question one's beliefs.
Another thing – her smell of chickenfeed.
To be precise, of chickenfeed and lemon.
Curled up on my eiderdown this morning,
she looked like something put there to annoy me –
and I must admit I felt a strong temptation
to wring her little neck, and dispose of her,
which would have been quite easy in the circumstances,
there being no bright feathers to betray us.

Carnations

And when he died, the reign of brutality and abuse
that had gone on undetected for nearly twenty years
suddenly came to an end;
and we fell asleep among our fathers' horses,
and that's how it all began –
with the sound of their breathing.
They waited by our sides, like aeroplanes,
or graves, enclosed in silk,
dusty and sweet like sponge cakes
or carnations;
we must have lain exhausted at their feet
for many days and nights;
we saw the moon
unroll ten thousand miles of suffering
along their backs, as if the mane of one alone
were Upper Burma,
as if each fetlock were Mongolia,
where there's only fifty miles of tarmacked road,
the rest's small flowers...
What happened next, my friend,
you already know –
something it's hard for the people here to believe,
after the reign of abuse
we've been subjected to,
timid as we are,
for so long now.

Evelyn

All I do's admire the distant sky-line
and run my fingers through the rustly sand
while Evelyn, ever patient and resourceful,
trundles off in search of tasty ants.
And every night, at peace beneath the stars,
we visualise the zoo-man in his bedroom
battling with his large electric fan.
We visualise him getting out of bed
and switching off, not only his supply,
but everyone's. The whole population's.
And everything goes ominously quiet.
Then gradually, as dawn begins to break,
he sees to his astonishment brown animals
shuffling up his drive with their families;
and as the days go by he gets to like them
– in fact he can't imagine ever not.
They fill his house and gardens with their
normalness. Just the way they seem so down-to-earth.

Marguerite

Because of the execution or suicide
of so many of his intimates,

they are looking with mounting desperation
for someone who really knew him –

someone who knew the place
where he held the meetings,

who had seen his face;
someone who fed him,

mashed the flesh of his apples;
replaced his warm lilies;

who tiptoed across the bright fence
in her checked dress

with a convoy of lorries
rumbling through her heart.

That person is me.
But nothing will induce me to come forward.

I will stay here in the ruins of the hospital
with Marguerite, the one I love,

who has not forgiven me for going away before,
and will not forgive me again. Not a day passes

without my sitting quietly by her cage
as if to apologise.

The people on the island bring her meat
caught in the woods for her.

These are the men with disabilities,
who feel respect for such a proud creature.

And those confined to wheelchairs can sing praises to her
streamlined silhouette.

The Hare

Beside the river in the dead of night,
a cry, and then another, like a spell,
turns the darkened beeches into light,
the silence of the woods into a bell;
and in the cottage on the moonlit hill
a woman shivers in her narrow bed
to hear the hare; and then the hare is still;
she feels its dusty fur against her head,
its ginger paws, that panic like trapped flies,
or tiny fish that see, or sense, dry land;
she feels it move; she hears its wild cries
glittering inside her ear like sand:
he's lost inside the forest of her hair,
and finds, and steals, his mother's kisses there.

Voices of Bulgaria

He's found a bear the same size as his mother
and walks about the dayroom holding her.
He calls her Marigold. With velvet ears

he hears the yellow sea below the window
rocking on the sand-bar like a horse
lying on its side, that can't stand up;

or like the parrot that he slept beside:
he wrapped it in a scarf with hearts on it,
to keep it warm, but even then it died...

His heavy hand is resting on her dress,
crushing her dumb sleepy whitened roots
beneath the snow, beside the little villa,

where lost mysterious voices of Bulgaria
are heard among the rabbits, quietly singing...
He grunts and ties his hair into a knot.

The polystyrene granules Marigold
was holding back so long come pouring down
like gold and jewels: *Marigold, my love!*

Marylou

She must have been extremely tired that morning,
and, as far as we can picture her today,
she must have been relieved to see the hut
she came to know so intimately later.

He would have been at work on the verandah,
completely dressed, as usual, in brown fur,
his human face half-hidden by his mask.
She watched him for a while, from a distance,

then something scared her, and she slipped away,
keeping close to where the river ran,
and planning to return with reinforcements,
with – sadly, as it turned out – Marylou.

The days that followed must have been the happiest,
certainly the quietest, of their lives –
the flickering fire, the dice, the racks of mushrooms,
the snow that watched them from the porch like dolls.

My Darling Reindeer

I was still feeling wary of humans, as you know,
and my first reaction was one of profound relief.
The sun came out, and everthing went quiet.
Once a tiny aeroplane flew over,
otherwise the only sound was crickets
clicking in the asters like dry nuts.
And then a man appeared, as if from nowhere,
and sat beside us, like a normal man,
like long ago, when there were people here,
and hungry men, and dogs; and crackly radios
competed with the crickets' castanets.

Hundreds of Letters to Hundreds of Naked Men

When he comes home in the evening
and stands in their bedroom
like a police officer at low tide
beside the clock
the thief threw into the sea
he hasn't noticed yet
because of the crabs and shoes and guillemot corpses
like hundreds of strewn-about letters
to hundreds of naked men,
she can't even look
without wanting to shrivel him up;
without wanting her look,
like the relentless sun
that renders bared farms
salt-encrusted wasteland
good for nothing but racing racing-cars on,
to shrivel him up.

But on the day they called him out three times,
as the only practising apiarist in the area,
she suddenly felt as if they had fallen in love,
she suddenly felt as if they were lovers again
(his lip on her neck,
their love in the air like a lark),
but it was no more alive than the dachshund
she met one night in the cul-de-sac,
lark-coloured,
and soft as a bean-pod lining,
that had died there –
everyone knows that –
that had died there,
swaying its final,
disappointed, spurious,
amber sway,
O, *years* ago.

Sparkle

I'm not as unprepared as you might think.
Take a look outside my window. *Dogs.*
All day they wait like soldiers for my voice,
a voice so beautiful that everyone –
no, not so beautiful, a voice so clear –
that everyone who hears it, dogs included,
will leave the hospital, without a fuss,
some with chocolates, some with fish, or fruit,
and make their way into the distant mountains.
And if they want to dress in dresses, let them.

Let them wear the shiniest materials
the nurses and the clergy can provide,
so when they reach their final destination
the rocks will sparkle with them – for one year.
Then men will come, attracted by the light,
and, armed with flames, expertly incinerate them;
returning with the ash to the valley,
where things have changed, and even dogs are burnt,
and palm trees' desiccated leaves go clacketty,
in at the hospital windows, *clacketty-clack.*

The Voice of Bobo

(i.m. the late Bobo, bull terrier)

Everything inside this room is mine.
And everyone inside it has to stay.

It's where I keep my horses and my men,
cooled on summer days by giant fans

whose steady rhythm
calms the anxious mind.

Nor do I want torpor, or docility.
From the very moment I arrive

I like to have each person's full attention,
until a silence is attained so deep

some of you will hear the Voice of Bobo,
when, after having queues of tiresome people

teasing her by blowing down her ear,
she suddenly can't bear it any longer

and starts to bark, as only Bobo can.
Those who hear that precious Voice go forward

to other, smaller rooms, for the Advanced.
Everybody else must stay on here –

here between the land and the sea
where long ago I built this secret palace

balanced on the cliff among the predators
to take advantage of the sweeping views.

Abstract Expressionism

She had this huge dog –
a mastiff, I think it was,
that her father had bought her
when the doctor suggested having a dog might help –
and she walked very fast on her spindly legs beside him,
trying to keep up; she'd come up alongside him finally,
and he'd stare into her eyes
like Wittgenstein.
It was snowing – the sort of weather,
the harbour-master said,
one minute you were wishing you were dying,
the next minute you were wishing that you weren't;
and the girl with the big dog laughed,
although she didn't understand him,
and she was only wearing a cardigan,
so she must have been terribly cold.
Then the harbour-master
invited her into his little office,
where two German tourists,
looking very much at home, were painting the sea.
Was it you who was saying, the bigger one said,
Ad Reinhardt went all the way round the world
and took 5000 photographs – or was it 50,000? –
and not a single one of a human,
not a single one!
Her partner nodded, and gave the dog a sandwich,
and then looked up at the owner,
who got one too.

Sips

They come from certain over-heated quarries
that operate illicitly, in relays,
for those who are attracted to the flowers
that grow gigantic in the noonday sun.

And then they come on here and pester me –
sort of pester, sort of guide my lips
until, like them, I learn to sip the flowers
that grow so big they block the daylight out,

and people are condemned to live in darkness;
and, such is their confusion, every day
men with yellow dogs patrol the rocks
and kill and quarter anything that moves.

Night-Night

I met him on the stairs quite unexpectedly,
and there and then I left the little hospital
and, trusting him as much, or more, than humans,
followed him, without a word – to you.
Some of you, I know, have been expecting us,
have waited years, in fact, for our arrival,
so can I take this opportunity
of thanking you for your encouragement?
Your country, as you know, is not well liked,
and anyone who comes, must come alone.
We have to make our way across the mountains
by intuition, some would say mistake,
not really knowing why we started out,
or who we are, or what we're looking for.
It's like the special side-room at the hospital
that patients other patients were unsettled by,
patients needing quiet, used to sleep in.
And people loathed it. Anything but that!
Why? Because it's up a little stair,
and looking out on nothing but the moors.
But once they did, and this applied to everyone,
a subtle transformation would come over them.

Wolves

Normally a rather timid man,
he knew exactly what he had to do –
find a wolf, and, watching every movement,
kneel down before her in the darkness
where endless little bands of beady nightlife
stream like gold across the forest floor
as if there's been some terrible mistake
that only they are able to correct,
only they and those like them who know.
Most of all, he needed to kneel down –
something not encouraged in an office.
Offices are not the place for tiptoeing,
gazing, kneeling, anything like that.
Offices are not the place for wolves,
or anyone involved with them, or night.
Offices are meant for office-workers.
Anybody else will be removed
and flattened out in basements by machines.
Nothing is the name they'll be remembered by,
lots of it, as ordered, nice and flat.

The Island

Men want to understand, and think they do,
and maybe if they don't it's not their fault,
but basically this place belongs to us.
We like to organise ourselves ourselves.
And anyway, anyone can visit –
brothers, fathers, lovers, anyone.
My son comes often; or I visit him.
You ask us if we miss them. Not at all.
We don't use cars, or electricity,
and men especially seem to find that hard.
Another thing – we feel healthier.
We work the horses; bear much fewer children;
and eat and dress and live very simply.
We shepherd sheep. We scale trees for fruit.
We abseil cliffs for samphire and fresh eggs;
and some of us, as you have pointed out,
migrating to the cities, abseil glass.

Heatwave

(for Heywood and Jenny)

Only the movement of the occasional rabbit
or the drifting shadow of a distant crow
disturbed the stillness of the marble quarry;
and it must have been nearly an hour, he told me later,
before he saw her, white against the grass –

white as fish-bones,
white as sun-bleached eyelashes,
white as the elongated mother-of-pearl lozenges
cunningly inlaid in the musical cigarette-box of her second home,
white as the hands of the man who delivers her anthracite beans.

What Happens in the Present

Why do they have to have their fried eggs and black coffee and tame
        maids
and an urgent phone-call to make,
and not enough time to time time?
And are their holidays really relaxed enough?
And are the shops near enough?
And the car servile enough?
And is the moment following the moment
following the moment fast enough?

so they never get touched by the present's immediate present –
where women walk to beaches with white skin;
where the beach-chalets' very decay
lends them an air of sanctity we feel at home in;
where salt smells of salt;
where silk feels like topspin;
where people we pass belong to the same side as we do,
where everyone does;

where a briefcase sits alone in a locked office
as its owner comes crawling along a narrow ledge five storeys up
to get it back, and carry it home through the streets to his strip-lit bed
where bagfuls of kittens mew from nightbound skips;
where someone like me – for the sake of the way things are,
for the sake of the present,
for the sake of its calm, enigmatic compassion –
will die for someone like you.

How To Be Happy

In the crowded hold of someone's boat,
chocolate sauce is being poured on pears
that shudder as the chocolate coats their shoulders
and spreads its lip across each tilted plate,
across the laps of guests, the rubber floor,
till everything is sunk in utter darkness,
and no one speaks, and no one even moves.
Years go by; then someone's eyes make out
the polished surface of a chocolate sea
where tiny golden boats are busy fishing.

Boating

Few, if any, went to bed that night,
and in the morning rescue teams set out.
Only those too weak to help remained –
the little man, the children, three small hens.
They waited in the house for what seemed days
until a river made of melting snow
carried them away towards the sea –
everyone, that is, except the man,
who had a boat, and rowed upstairs to bed,
but even that, his fifty-year-old bed;
slipped away as he approached, like sand,
and then the house itself was washed away,
and he was left to roam the world alone,
rowing through the tree-tops in his nightshirt,
or sometimes rowing, sometimes simply drifting,
feeling too relaxed to really think;
but once he saw a woman dressed in white
waving from the rail of a liner;
but when he called, she didn't answer him –
as if to stop him calling out like that
and spoiling the whole joy of the occasion.

Eating Lychees in South Kensington

Still blushing at the feet of tall men's houses —
fathers' and uncles' chocolate-brown retreats

whose nephews tap the lighted streets, like roebuck
glittering with gold and tangerines;

blonde heirs made of knives for slicing veal;
or trout, that mirror water; polished beans —

she feels, in her pocket, crenellations
of waterfalls that she begins to eat:

their sweet, shelled, oval-headed babies
crush their juicy mouths against her cheek;

and chandeliers, as fresh as shrimps and oranges,
clatter in her jaw; while on the street,

she hears, like falling snow, pink in the sunlight,
the sound of gathering armies' naked feet.

A Nightdress Sprinkled with Fish Scales

After what the family call 'the accident'
my sister brought me here to this small castle
that rises from the shores of a lake
rumoured to be one of the deepest,
certainly the clearest, in the country.
And when I say I fish 'from my bed'
I mean exactly that. Have a look.
Swimming may no longer be an option
but fishing is. I lay them on my bed,
cold and heavy like abandoned guns,
and tell myself how fortunate I am.
The doctor, quite a fisherman himself,
sometimes finds a scale, like confetti,
sticking to my nightdress or my bandages,
and picks them carefully off, like tiny mirrors,
before he turns away to join the swimmers
fanning out across my bedside lake.

The Postman Like a Bunch of Flowers

The women on the quay call him Crocodile
and shower him with stones and bits of glass.
They ought to call him something nice like Flowers.
He doesn't even eat the local fish.
Far less meat. Far less other people.
He's much too busy caring for the fruit
whose strange imported colours block the highway –
their wild reds, their toxic-looking purples,
their pinks and blues, like little tensed-up babies
he dreams at night of taking in his arms
and rocking in a light but steady rhythm
until they fall, or drift, into a trance,
like furless pigs that loll about in barns
with eyelashes so white they are excused
any kind of action except sleep.

Mirabelle

I sit up here and watch them from my window
setting off, in groups of two or three,

across the miles of undulating concrete
to spend the day in what, for them, 's like prayer

retiring when night falls to giant pipes
that echo to the crunch of broken lambs

and something else I can't identify,
a distant pumping, like machines, or blood.

I watch, and wait for Mirabelle to come,
to press against the chainlink fence with orchids

and show me, in his way,
how much loves me.

We'll lie together like two hired snakes,
our brains as soft as sugar, or the skater

whose lovely fragile bones were ground to powder
and scattered on the sites of his despair.

The Veil

Otherwise the room was dark and empty,
except for what I took to be the servant,
apparently not bothered by the smell
I noticed straightaway, of blood and bleeding.
Her face was sullen, and she didn't move.
And neither did the rigid man-shaped veil.
After that, I came back every day,
until at last my patience was rewarded.
The veil moved – as if some furtive moths
were arguing among themselves like thieves.
As morning broke, I crept a little closer;
then, just as I was leaning down to speak,
the servant gave me one of those bleak looks
the neighbours have been paralysed by lately.
Not only you, my friends. The whole area.

Brueghel's Helicopter

The trees are white,
the hunters have gone home,
and even the skaters on the distant ponds
have fallen silent in the swirling snow.
The little pig has trotted back inside
and settled sweetly in my arms again;
and as it sleeps, its chin against my chest,
the bewildering adventures of the morning
come rushing back in all their vividness –
the way the mules flickered in the moonlight;
the glimmer of the cockpit in the rocks;
and finally the shock of seeing the pilot,
his chin against the window like white meat.

As dusk, then darkness, fall, and rumours spread,
people start to gather at the inn.
I hear the muffled crunch of their boots,
and then the stamps, as they approach the porch.
The men look cold,
their skinny dogs fed-up.
The only comfort I can offer's tea,
brewed by burning tables and dried flowers.
The piglet in my arms is fast asleep;
and one by one, as dawn breaks with no news,
each man returns for solace to his dreams:
I watch the snow, and dream of San Diego,
sizzling in the sun, and full of schnapps.

A Cup of Kindness

Reindeer calve; the dotterel
sings in the sedge like tin;

small Lapps net chard, and white milk
mixed with sorrel sours in kegs;

a baby, sucking bones in a willow-bush
is dreaming in a world of fur and cloud;

while, overhead, two patient botanists
try and remember the words of *Auld Lang Syne.*

Our Lady of Snow

The person in front of her's blood
continues to drip. The last thing she ate,
or anyone else in the party,
were the little roast breasts of a songbird
aeons ago. Her remaining arm
is difficult to move. She wonders
if they're trying hard enough. Or maybe a rescue
is somehow no longer the point,
and even those in pain – it's conceivable –
imagining the faces of their relatives,
the hospitals and diets and machines,
would rather stay on here in the mountains,
drinking snow, and watching for a plane;
and, as the days go by, no longer watching;
or watching without hope, or knowing why.
Perhaps it doesn't matter if she dies.
Perhaps it means the others will survive.
Her headless body will be rationed out,
to certain people, people who are mobile,
who'll move away, and build a new society,
far from where the rooms are buckled metal,
the beds are other people, or their limbs,
and walking has to be conducted slowly,
like walking with no shoes on on wet fish.

The Villa

His famous cock
that he goes on about's
about as much fun
as a frozen lamb,
and I just ran away
across the heath
one night;
I left the moonlit villa
far behind,
the helicopters, chainsaws,
parrots, knives,
and little maids who specialise
(he gives them sweets)
in screaming
at the parrots;
I slipped away,
and came back
here,
to you:
breathing gently
like a giant flower
smelling of custard
being stirred,
and licked –
custard
made of eggs
and warm vanilla pods
where egg-white islands
shunt
their sugar bays.

Orchids

The aeroplane must have been there
for several weeks. A few birds
were absent-mindedly picking through
the mangled remains of small children,
and a gold dog ran in and out
of the empty cabin, cradling
a spotted quince in its mouth.
The man we were looking for
was lying on a day-bed
under a red tree.
He seemed to be having some problem
with his skin, and was wearing
a pair of white silk gloves
and a white blood-stained hat.
He was the only survivor able to speak
and even he was too weak to talk
for more than a few minutes at a time.
He was an ex-oil-pipe-contractor
and a millionaire
who had been looking for a place
to breed orchids...and as he spoke
he lay back on the bleached canvas
of his ancient bed,
his eyes beginning to run,
his limp white penis
resting in the sunlight
on his glove. While my colleague
went in search of a blanket,
I listened to the gunfire
from the valley,
where my daughter lay awake
behind closed curtains
guarded by sweet machines
like a rare flower.

The Runway

As days, then weeks, went by,
my fears increased.
Once a hare was taken from a trap;
once I heard the crunch of a boot.
Finally, late one afternoon,
walking back along the upper bank,
I saw a swimmer swim across the lake.
I watched him for a little while in silence,
then gathered stones and stoned him steadily
until he disappeared without a trace,
and silence re-established itself – .
silence, and the memory of Mother,
zipped up in her nylon sleeping-bag,
dragging herself slowly like a foot
across the tarmac with a scraping sound.